The CLEAR and SIMPLE Workbooks

I Can Read!

Grade 1
Sight Words

By Nancy Jolson Leber & Liane B. Onish

Grosset & Dunlap

Cover Design by Traci Levine

Interior Design by Susan LiCalsi Design

Cover and Interior Illustrations by Robin Boyer

GROSSET & DUNLAP

Published by the Penguin Group

Penguin Group (USA) Inc., 375 Hudson Street, New York, New York 10014, U.S.A.

Penguin Group (Canada), 90 Eglinton Avenue East, Suite 700, Toronto, Ontario, Canada M4P 2Y3
(a division of Pearson Penguin Canada Inc.)

Penguin Books Ltd, 80 Strand, London WC2R 0RL, England

Penguin Ireland, 25 St Stephen's Green, Dublin 2, Ireland
(a division of Penguin Books Ltd)

Penguin Group (Australia), 250 Camberwell Road, Camberwell, Victoria 3124, Australia
(a division of Pearson Australia Group Pty Ltd)

Penguin Books India Pvt Ltd, 11 Community Centre, Panchsheel Park, New Delhi - 110 017, India

Penguin Group (NZ), Cnr Airborne and Rosedale Roads, Albany, Auckland 1310, New Zealand
(a division of Pearson New Zealand Ltd)

Penguin Books (South Africa) (Pty) Ltd, 24 Sturdee Avenue, Rosebank, Johannesburg 2196, South Africa

Penguin Books Ltd, Registered Offices:
80 Strand, London WC2R 0RL, England

ISBN 0-448-44127-6   10 9 8 7 6 5 4 3 2 1

Dear Parents,

Clear and Simple Workbooks are designed to support you in guiding your emerging reader. Reading is essential to academic success. About 70 to 80 percent of children are able to break the sound/letter code after one year of instruction. Your first-grader can get ready by practicing the sounds that letters stand for (phonics), as well as learning sight words that do not follow regular spelling patterns and, therefore, cannot be sounded out.

Did you know?

- **Explicit, systematic phonics instruction is a successful way to teach young or slow-to-learn readers.**

- **Seeing a word while simultaneously hearing or saying it helps to spell it. Activities that focus on the structure of words help create visual images, which children will then use as they read and write. Self-correction is the single greatest factor in learning to spell.**

- **One-third of all our writing in English is made up of just 31 words! Learning to automatically recognize these words is critical for reading fluency.**

The skills needed for reading are complex, but Clear and Simple Workbooks make these skills . . . clear and simple. Each page introduces a phonics skill and a key picture, or a high-frequency word with reading and writing practice. Clear and Simple Workbooks make learning fun and easy for your child. Here's how:

- The simple, consistent design and the repetitive, patterned activities are predictable enough so that your child can use the books independently. In *Let's Sound Out Words*, your child will learn sound/letter relationships. In *I Can Read!*, your child will trace, read, and write new words and will then discriminate among different words and practice writing. Before long, your child will be able to identify direction words, such as *circle* and *color*.

- Clear and Simple Workbooks reinforce the new skills your child practices by providing storybooks in which words are repeated in a context your child can relate to.

- Some activities are open-ended, allowing for multiple correct answers as children work at their own level and feel successful. Furthermore, the review storybooks allow for creativity as your child will finish writing a page and illustrating it.

- Use Clear and Simple Workbooks as an opportunity for you and your child to spend quality time together. Have your child explain the pages to you and discuss the pictures. Get started by reading the first couple of pages aloud and working together. Provide crayons and pencils, along with a lot of support and praise.

Reading is the most important academic skill your child will learn. Make reading a positive, playful family experience using the Clear and Simple Workbook series.

Happy reading,

Nancy Jolson Leber

Nancy Jolson Leber
Educational Consultant

Liane B. Onish

Liane B. Onish
Educational Consultant

These are the sight words your child will practice in this book. To pre-test, have your child try to read each word on the list below. Put a check mark in the BEFORE column next to the ones your child knows. Then after completing the book, have your child read the words again. Put a check mark in the AFTER column.

BEFORE	WORD LIST	AFTER
	and	
	the	
	to	
	was	
	said	
	are	
	they	
	good	
	with	
	have	
	on	
	off	
	for	
	you	
	one	
	all	
	up	
	down	
	yes	
	no	
	me	
	my	
	at	
	that	
	in	
	out	
	him	
	her	

and

👆 Say the letters as you trace the word above.

✏️ Trace and copy the word.

(Circle) your favorite!

and

Write **and** to finish the sentence.

I like peanut butter __ __ __ jelly.

Oral Language: Ask your child to name two things s/he likes. Then have your child finish and repeat the sentence: I like __ and __.

and

Read and trace the word above.

(Circle) two words in each row that are the same.

and	and	an
and	dim	and
add	and	and
and	am	and

Write the word and check it.

Cover it and write it again. Repeat.

the

 Say the letters as you trace the word above.

 Trace and copy the word.

(Circle) your favorite!

the

Write the to finish the sentence.

I pet ___ ___ ___ cat.

© 2006 Grosset & Dunlap

 Oral Language: Have your child name an animal to pet. Then have your child finish and repeat the sentence: I pet the ___.

the

✏️ Read and trace the word above.
Ⓒircle the three times to win tic-tac-toe.

the	then	the
the	this	the
that	there	the

✏️ Write the word and check it.
Cover it and write it again. Repeat.

to

 Say the letters as you trace the word above.

 Trace and copy the word.

(Circle) your favorite!

to

Write to to finish the sentence.

I like ___ ___ read.

Oral Language: Ask your child to name something s/he likes to do. Then have your child finish and repeat the sentence: I like to ___.

to

Read and trace the word above.

(Circle) the word **to** six times.

a	t	s	k	f	t
t	o	p	n	o	j
g	o	t	o	h	e
u	t	o	b	i	w
f	o	k	a	t	o
b	a	r	l	o	d

Write the word and check it.

Cover it and write it again. Repeat.

was

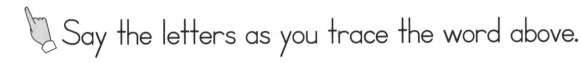

Say the letters as you trace the word above.

Trace and copy the word.

(Circle) your favorite!

was

Write **was** to finish the sentence.

The 🎡 ___ ___ ___ fun!

Oral Language: Ask your child to name a ride s/he liked. Then have your child finish and repeat the sentence: The ___ was fun.

Read and trace the word above.

Color the spaces with the word was.

Write the word and check it.

Cover it and write it again. Repeat.

The Bus

It was 8!

Fluency: Help your child read the book. Then have your child reread.

Jack **and** Zack ran **to the** bus.

The bus **was** late!

 **Circle** the sentence that tells what happens next.

Jack **and** Zack get on **the** bus.

Jack **and** Zack miss **the** bus.

 Comprehension: Have your child draw a picture to go with the circled sentence.

16

said

 Say the letters as you trace the word above.

Trace and copy the word.

(Circle) your favorite!

said

Write said to finish the sentence.

She said, "Hello!"   He __ __ __ __, "Hi."

Oral Language: Ask your child whom s/he talks to. Then have your child finish and repeat the sentence: I said, "__" to __.

17

said

Read and trace the word above.

Circle two words in each row that are the same.

said	sad	said
sail	said	said
said	said	sad
sold	said	said

Write the word and check it.

Cover it and write it again. Repeat.

are

Say the letters as you trace the word above.

Trace and copy the word.

(Circle) your favorite!

are

Write are to finish the sentence.

We ___ ___ ___ riding.

© 2006 Grosset & Dunlap

Oral Language: Ask your child what s/he does with a friend. Then have your child finish and repeat the sentence: (Name) and I are ___ .

are

✏️ Read and trace the word above.
(Circle) are three times to win tic-tac-toe.

are	are	arm
art	are	are
ran	and	are

✏️ Write the word and check it.
Cover it and write it again. Repeat.

they

👆 Say the letters as you trace the word above.

✏️ Trace and copy the word.

（Circle） your favorite!

they

Write **They** to finish the sentence.

__ __ __ __ like to hop!

Oral Language: Ask your child how two friends have fun. Then have your child finish and repeat the sentence: They like to __ .

they

Read and trace the word above.

(Circle) the word they five times.

```
t  h  e  y  f  t
h  o  p  n  o  h
e  t  h  e  y  e
y  t  h  b  i  y
t  h  e  y  t  o
b  o  y  t  h  e
```

Write the word and check it.

Cover it and write it again. Repeat.

good

 Say the letters as you trace the word above.

Trace and copy the word.

(Circle) your favorite!

good

Write good to finish the sentence.

The is __ __ __ __ !

HOME Oral Language: Ask your child to name something good to eat. Then have your
child finish and repeat the sentence: __ is good.

✏️ Read and trace the word above.

🖍️ Color the spaces with the word good.

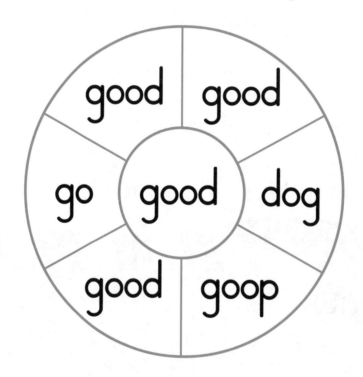

✏️ Write the word and check it.

Cover it and write it again. Repeat.

Yum!

"They are red," said Gail.

"They are sweet," said Kate.

Fluency: Help your child read the book. Then have your child reread.

25

"They are small," said Gail.
"Seeds are inside," said Kate.

"They are good to eat!" said Gail.
"Yum!" said Kate.

🖊 (Circle) the correct picture.

strawberries

cherries

watermelon

They are ___ .

HOME

Comprehension: Have your child draw and write an ending to the story.

with

Say the letters as you trace the word above.

Trace and copy the word.

(Circle) your favorite!

with

Write **with** to finish the sentence.

I sail ___ ___ ___ ___ Dad.

Oral Language: Ask your child what s/he likes to do. Then have your child finish and repeat the sentence: I ___ with (Name).

with

✏️ Read and trace the word above.

(Circle) two words in each row that are the same.

with	wit	with
mitt	with	with
with	with	wide
will	with	with

✏️ Write the word and check it.

Cover it and write it again. Repeat.

have

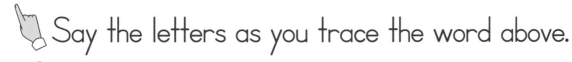

Say the letters as you trace the word above.

Trace and copy the word.

(Circle) your favorite!

have

Write have to finish the sentence.

I __ __ __ __ a big dog!

Oral Language: Ask your child to name something s/he has. Then have your child finish and repeat the sentence: I have a ___ .

31

have

✏️ Read and trace the word above.

(Circle) have three times to win tic-tac-toe.

have	hive	hair
hate	have	love
name	here	have

✏️ Write the word and check it.

Cover it and write it again. Repeat.

on   off

 Say the letters as you trace the words above.

 Trace and copy the words.

on

off

Write on and off to finish the sentences.

She is ___ ___ .

He is ___ ___ ___ .

Oral Language: Invite your child to use **on** and **off** in sentences.

33

on   off

✏️ Read and trace the words above.

Find and (circle) the words on and off.

Can you find at least three of each?

o	n	y	k	f	o
a	o	p	w	o	f
d	n	j	e	s	f
c	e	o	f	f	y
l	b	t	o	f	f
o	f	f	l	o	n

✏️ Write each word you circled.

Cover it and write it again. Check.

_____   _____

- - - - - - - - - -   - - - - - - - - - -

_____   _____

- - - - - - - - - -   - - - - - - - - - -

_____   _____

for you

 Say the letters as you trace the words above.

 Trace and copy the words.

for

you

Write for and you to finish the sentences.

Is it __ __ __ me?

It is __ __ __ __ __ __ !

Oral Language: **Challenge** your child to use **for** and **you** in one sentence.

Read and trace the words above.

Color the spaces with **for** in red.

Color the spaces with **you** in yellow.

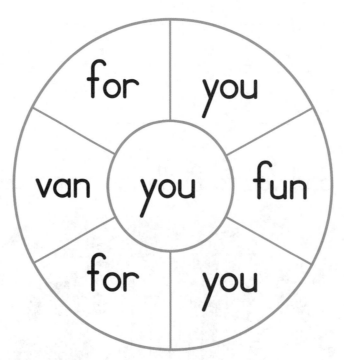

Write each word you colored.

Cover it and write it again. Check.

_____   _____

- - - - - - - - - - - - - -   - - - - - - - - - - - - - -

_____   _____

- - - - - - - - - - - - - -   - - - - - - - - - - - - - -

_____   _____

For Us!

"Can **you** go **with** us?" Mike asked.
"I **have** to ask Mom," I said.

Fluency: Help your child read the book. Then have your child reread.

37

"You can go **with** Mike," said Mom.
"Slip this **on.**"

"I will take this **off**," said Bo.

"Can I see what **you have**?" asked Mike.

"I have _____ for us!" said Bo.

HOME

Comprehension: Have your child draw what Bo has in the box. Then your child can write what will happen next.

one all

 Say the letters as you trace the words above.

 Trace and copy the words.

 one

all

Write one and all to finish
the sentences.

I have ___ ___ ___ .

I have ___ ___ ___ the .

 Comprehension: Have your child circle all the dogs; make an X on one; draw the boy with at least one leash.

one   all

Read and trace the words above.

(Circle) two words in each row that are the same.

one	on	one
all	all	call
or	one	one
ill	all	all

Write each word you circled.
Cover it and write it again. Check.

up   down

 Say the letters as you trace the words above.

 Trace and copy the words.

up

down

Write up and down to finish the sentences.

He is ___ ___.

She is ___ ___ ___ ___.

 Oral Language: Have your child draw him/herself in the picture. Ask your child to finish and repeat the sentence: I am ___. (up or down)

up down

Read and trace the words above.

(Circle) up three times.

(Circle) down three times.

Which word wins tic-tac-toe?

down	down	up
dawn	up	us
up	down	own

Write each word you circled.

Cover it and write it again. Check.

yes no

Say the letters as you trace the words above.

Trace and copy the words.

yes

no

Write the sentences with Yes or No.

___ ___ ___! ___ ___ ___! ___ ___ ___!

___ ___! ___ ___! ___ ___!

© 2006 Grosset & Dunlap

HOME

Oral Language: Ask your child questions with **yes** or **no** answers. Then invite your child to ask you questions.

Read and trace the words above.

Find and circle the words yes and no.

Can you find at least four of each?

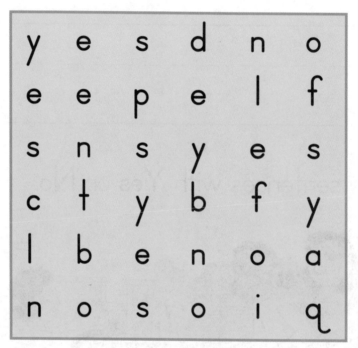

y	e	s	d	n	o
e	e	p	e	l	f
s	n	s	y	e	s
c	t	y	b	f	y
l	b	e	n	o	a
n	o	s	o	i	q

Write each word you circled.

Cover it and write it again. Check.

me my

 Say the letters as you trace the words above.

 Trace and copy the words.

me

my

Write me and my to finish the sentences.

This is ___ ___ .

This is ___ ___ .

 Oral Language: Have your child use **me** and **my** in sentences.

47

me   my

Read and trace the words above.

Color the spaces with **me** in green.

Color the spaces with **my** in red.

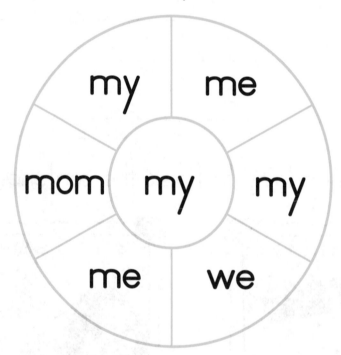

Write each word you colored.

Cover it and write it again. Check.

The Slide

My dad and I went to a park.
Look at **all** the fun, wet things!

Fluency: **Help your child read the book. Then have your child reread.**

"Can I go **all** the way **up**?" I asked.
"**Yes.** Go with **me**," said Dad.

"Can we go **down**?" I asked.
"Oh, **no**!" said Dad.

"Yes!" I said.

"Okay. Just **one** time!" said Dad.

_____

- -

_____

Comprehension: Have your child draw and write what will happen next.

at   that

 Say the letters as you trace the words above.

 Trace and copy the words.

at

that

Write at and that to finish the sentences.

Look at __ __ __ __ hit!

Grace is __ __ first base.

 Oral Language: Invite your child to draw him/herself in the picture. Then have your child finish and repeat the sentence with **at** or **that**: I am ___ the game.

at   that

✏️ Read and trace the words above.
Ⓒircle two words in each row that are the same.

at	that	at
that	that	hat
it	at	at
that	than	that

✏️ Write each word you circled.
Cover it and write again. Check.

in out

 Say the letters as you trace the words above.

Trace and copy the words.

in

out

Write in and out to finish the sentences.

She is ___ ___ ___ .

He is ___ ___ .

Oral Language: Invite your child to draw a cat in the picture. Then have your child finish and repeat the sentence with **in** or **out**: The cat is ___.

in out

Read and trace the words above.

(Circle) in three times.

(Circle) out three times.

Which word wins tic-tac-toe? _____

at	in	out
in	off	out
in	that	out

Write each word you circled.

Cover it and write it again. Check.

_____   _____

_____   _____

_____   _____

56

him   her

 Say the letters as you trace the words above.

 Trace and copy the words.

him

her

Write him and her to finish the sentences.

He can sing to __ __ __ .

She can dance for __ __ __ .

 Oral Language: Ask your child to use **him** or **her** in sentences.

✏️ Read and trace the words above.

Find and (circle) the words him and her.

Can you find four of each?

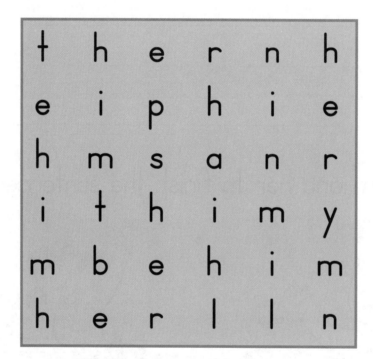

t	h	e	r	n	h
e	i	p	h	i	e
h	m	s	a	n	r
i	t	h	i	m	y
m	b	e	h	i	m
h	e	r	l	l	n

✏️ Write each word you circled.

Cover it and write it again. Check.

Out, Spot!

Spot is in the tub.
It is time to get out.

HOME

Fluency: Help your child read the book. Then have your child reread.

Bud and Spot are **at** the door.
"Stay **out** if you are wet," said Mom.

"Spot is not wet. Look!" Bud said to **her**.
"Is **that** right?" Mom asked.

Comprehension: Have your child draw and write what will happen next.

I Can Read!

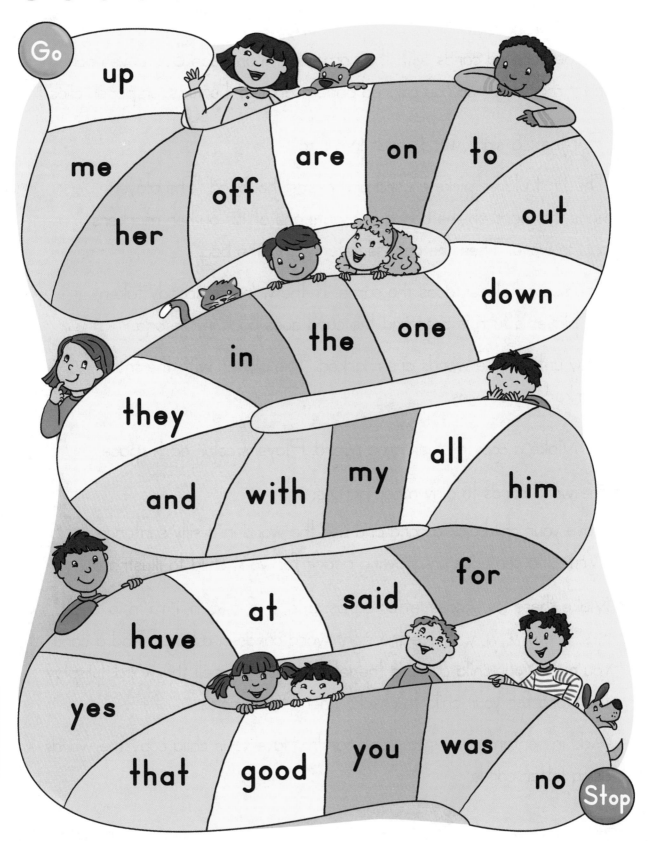

Go

up

me

off

her

are

on

to

out

down

in

the

one

they

and

with

my

all

him

have

at

said

for

yes

that

good

you

was

no

Stop

See how to play on page 64.

Fun and Games

Use the perforated cards with the game board on page 63. Give each player 14 markers, such as colored paper squares, buttons, or paper clips.

1. Put the 28 sight word cards in a bag.

2. The first player picks a card and reads the word. The player finds the word on the board and puts one of his or her markers on the word. Then the card is returned to the bag.

3. The second player does the same. If the word is already taken, the player's turn is over and the card goes back in the bag.

4. Play until all the words are marked. The player with the most marked words wins.

Option: Make a copy of the game board. Players color each space.

Use the word cards to play other games:

- Have your child pick a card and use the word in a silly sentence. Write the sentence on drawing paper for your child to illustrate.

- Make these lowercase letter cards: a, d, e, f, f, g, h, i, m, n, o, o, p, r, s, t, t, u, v, w, y. Place the sight word cards in a bag. Read a card you pick. Your child can use the letter cards to spell the word. Display the word for your child to check. Then switch roles.

- Add important names to blank cards. Have your child copy the words using letter cards.

and	the	to	was
said	are	they	good
with	have	on	off
for	you	one	all

up	down	yes	no
me	my	at	that
in	out	him	her